# "A Few of My Favorite Things"

*A short book of poetry by G. Allegra Elam*

# Book Description:

Poems from the heart and mind, body and soul of a girl to a woman experiencing the highs and lows of this thing called "Life"

Copyright 2010 G. Allegra Elam

ISBN 978-0-578-05350-9

# A Few of My Favorite Things

*Poetry for the mind, body and soul*

*G. Allegra Elam*

*This book is dedicated to the memory of my beloved parents Sophie Reed Elam and Donald P. Elam, until we meet again, I will carry you in my heart...*

# Thanks...

To God: for loving me enough to give me this life, these hands, these eyes, this heart and mind... Your Mercy and Grace has indeed been sufficient!

To my family for being there, love ya Jean and Skeet!

To my friends (you know who you are) that have supported all of my dreams and have coached me down off the ledge when I've given up (lord knows that's more times than I even need to mention, LOL!), oh and least I forget, those friends who have answered the phone and heard me screaming "This is the worst day of my life!" you also know who you are...LOL!!! Smooches!

P.S. I am grateful and I love y'all!

This little chat book of poetry is a reflection of my emotions and feelings about people, places and things that have been a part of my learning, growing, and living.

I was in High School when I took a pen and pad and wrote down the words that would describe how I felt about music and Voila!, my first born work of art entitled, "All about the Music" and so it began...

I always feared that if I were to share my work, people would laugh or not think that it was good, but I realized that poetry is relative. My poetry is a window into *my* experiences in life, people *I've* met, and places *I've* been. My hope is that everyone who reads my work will find something in one of the poems that remind them of a place or a time when they could relate. Thank you for your support and love.

Special thanks to W.A.N for leaning on me to get this done...you're the King! LOL!

*-G Allegra Elam*

# "The Wonder Years..."

*All about the music*

*Day dreaming*

Okay, this was my first poem! I know it's short, but come on, I was a teenager already! LOL!

I was sitting on my front porch on one summer's eve and began to hum a little and sing. I took out my pen and pad and wrote exactly how I felt at that moment. It is simply about the music and its affect on people and the world we live in. I LOVE MUSIC!!!!!! It is like medicine to my soul.

-1982

# All about the music

*Music is happy, Music is sad*

*Music can often make me glad!*

*Music is here, Music is real*

*Music can make the earth stand still…*

My second poem...

One of my favorite pass times growing up was to day dream.
I would sit and think how wonderful it would be to escape for just
a moment and create a vision in your mind; it's the only time you
can have the perfect world you desire. As a child, I often played
alone and became quite creative. Daydreaming is also a great stress
reliever, try it sometimes....take a short trip...to an exotic place
you've never been, I dare you to dream!

-1982

# Day Dreaming

*Sometimes I sit and wonder*
*Though it doesn't matter where,*
*I don't know why I do it,*
*I just sit there and stare*

*I think about things that make the world go round,*
*How peaceful it is sometimes when you can't hear a sound*

*I watch the children laugh and play*
*As the birds and butterflies run away,*
*I call it day dreaming, dreaming of the day…*

# "Intrigue"

*Pretty Brown Eyes*

*Presence*

*Clever*

*Café Au Lait*

Have you ever met a man with brown eyes? Well, I have and they were one of the prettiest pair of eyes I think I had ever seen. Hence, the inspiration for this poem. The intensity of his glare and the mystery behind his character made for quite an interesting introduction. First impressions are lasting ones…

-1993

# Pretty Brown Eyes

*Pretty brown eyes, what do you hide?*
*A distant past?*
*A sorted present?*
*A hopeful future?*

*Pretty brown eyes so strong and courageous*
*Look at me! Carry me over to your side,*
*Dance with me by the flickering candle,*
*Move with me like the waves of the ocean*
*Lay with me like the sand on a beach*

*Pretty brown eyes, I can't escape their glare,*
*Every time I close my eyes they are still there...*

There are lots of people in this world with lots of attributes, but the one thing the stands out is...a person with presence. This person can walk in a room and command attention without seeking it. A person who possesses this quality always leaves a lingering air of intrigue and mystery.

-1995

# Presence

*Your presence commands my attention*

*Your presence enters my mind and takes me places I've never been*

*Your presence allows my emotions to dance to the beat of a silent drum*

*Your presence produces a melodic tune that brings calm to a raging storm*

*...Without your presence*
*There is only space...*

Much can be said about a man who is clever. This poem describes every man that has ever swept you off your feet. You can't remember where he came from or even how he got his foot in your door. Just like a smooth criminal, he sneaks up on you...and, before you know it your guard is down and you are vulnerable to every emotion you could imagine. If you are not careful, before you know it, you'll find yourself under attack.

-2002

# Clever

*There I was, minding my business when I ran into clever…yeahhhhhhh, there he was with his smooth talk and his Denzel walk*

*He worked diligently like a thief in the night, disguising his craft with the swiftness of a gazelle, and before I knew it I had been…what the hell?*

*I asked myself: Could this be? Who is he? And…Why me…? My impulses tell me to run, but my instinct tells me to confront this intruder face to face cautiously moving at a steady pace…*

*But how long can I live in my fortress thinking that clever will not find me again and open my heart, enter my soul, and take my love!*

*So here he is with his smooth talk and Denzel walk…because he's cleverrrrrrrr!!!!*

This poem is simply about connection and kindred spirits. Destiny is a powerful thing. They say you can choose your destiny, but I don't believe you can. I believe that people, places and things are all a part of an inevitable plan for your life; now, what I do believe is choosing to listen to your inner voice will determine your destination. The key is learning to listen.

-2003

# Destiny

---

*Oh! There you are,*

*I see you, do you see me?*
*I feel you, do you feel me?*

*There you go!*

*Were you here?*
*Was I there?*

*Shhhh…Listen!*

*What is it?*
*My heart, your drum*
*Your breath, my song*

*Look!*

*Your footprints, my impression*

*Our lives*
*Our paths*
*Our center*
*Our SOULS…*

I wrote this poem for a guy I was dating at the time. As you will soon see, it was clearly a sort of frisky and flirtatious attempt to make him smile. He loved it - I might add. This same smiley man ended up being a jerk and not worth the effort, but as they say – it is what it is, you live and you learn. In retrospect, he did me a huge favor.

Hasta la Vista baby!

-1997

# Café Au Lait

*Oooh my Cafe' Au Lait*
*Let me give you my cup*
*So you can fill it up*

*Oooh how mellow you make me feel*
*So hot and steamy, so rich and creamy*
*Damn! That Café Au Lait …um…um…um*

*I save you for me and only me and those intimate moments*
*And special occasions…um…um…um there I go getting those sensations*

*Your aroma soothes my soul and warms my body until I lose control*
*Oh No! I'm almost finished, my cup is now empty*
*My mind reassures me that when I need more there is plenty, plenty, plenty*

*Um…um…um, I can't go a day without my Cafe' Au Lait, so take my*
*cup and fill it up*

# "Whimsy"

*Escapade*

Everyone needs an escapade every now and then. It's a fun way to enjoy life. When things get hectic, what better way to take a brake then to escape to some far away place of tranquility...Why not invite someone special to share in the fantasy?

- Year unknown

# Escapade

*Come with me on this trip*

*You ask where? I say there*

*...There where the sun bronzes everything it touches...*

*Where the water quenches every thirst*

*Where the night comes down like a blanket and covers the earth*

*While the restless soul, the moon, and the stars dance together in slow rhythmic movements*

*Would you like to go?*

*You ask where? I say there*

# "Inspiration"

*The Journey*

*Wondrous*

*Lord help me to hold up*

This poem was written for someone I knew who was taking on a very important responsibility. It was the beginning of a new journey. It was a life altering decision and should have been a very humbling experience. It is not easy making the choice between the world and God. Often, people in this situation find themselves all alone. In order to remain strong you may have to take some things with you as you travel this lonely highway, but if you take the right instruments, it can make your life richer and as a result someone else's life better.

-2004

# The Journey

*The first step begins...your life as you knew it ends...ahhh what revelations, what new horizons and oh what new challenges await you...*

*Did you prepare? Or is your luggage bare? How did you know when and where you should go?*

*Now comes your test and you must be at your best, but just take "the journey" my friend because the possibilities are infinite and God's dominion and power has no limit.*

*You will need a few things along the way...pack humility for those times when you feel humiliated...*

*Take humbleness for those times when you bite off a little more than you can chew...*

*Patience when your hopes and dreams don't happen the way you wanted them to...*

*Always remember the experiences shared by those who have come before you...*

*Keep unconditional love in a safe place because you never know when you may have to pull it out for someone you have never met...*

*When "the journey" ends and you meet the maker and creator of all that's good and perfect, can you say? "I have done my best, I have done your will, my work is done and now I must rest"*

*But not until, there is work still...there are souls to save, lives to bless, and hearts to touch...*

*This anointing on your life will carry you through "the journey" and his words will resonate through the walls of your labor, "well done, well done...thy good and faithful son"*

I wrote this poem in the beginning of spring one day when I was sitting on a bench down on the mall in Washington, DC. As the poem reads, it was a perfect picture on a perfect day. I was inspired by the air, the sky, the birds, the trees, the leaves and the laughter of children playing all around me, a reminder that... some of the best things in life are free.

-2004

# Wondrous

*Birds that make melodious sounds,*
*Trees that sway, while their leaves dance on the ground,*
*Children laugh and play...just a perfect picture on this perfect day*

*As I walked and watched people stroll, I pondered on my role*
*What am I to do with these wondrous gifts...the creator gave me*
*Surely I can make music like the birds...and sway like the trees and I can even*
*Dance like the leaves...*

*I am a separate creation, with a mind of my own and so I move through this journey*
*Learning and growing and living my story...and each day giving God the glory*

If you have ever been through something in life and you had some upbringing in the Baptist church, then, you know when you can't go anywhere else and all else fails, God will never let you down. Sometimes faith is all you have to hold onto. This was written during a very difficult time in my life when all I could seem to do was cry. Nothing I did was working and friends were not around.

They say that sometimes God has to place you in a space all by yourself to make you see him clearly. My mama used to say, "Gertie, ain't no use in praying if you gone worry, and ain't no use in worrying if you gone pray". This is where I was at the time I wrote this poem...in that space all by myself. I came through this troubling time stronger and writing this poem was like therapy.

-1998

# Lord Help Me to Hold Up

*Lord, help me to hold up*
*I am weak and I am tired*
*Oh, I think I'm losing this race*
*But Lord give me strength to pick up my feet and steady my pace*

*Lord, help me to hold up*
*I am sad and my eyes are weeping*
*What seeds could I be reaping?*

*I don't know where to go, which road to take, which path to make*
*But Lord wipe my tears so that I may see…give me direction and guide my feet*

*Lord, help me to hold up*
*Give me another day for I know that I'm not all I can be*
*But take me and make me the instrument you intended me to be*

*Lord, help me to hold up!!!!*

# "Identity"

*Who Am I?*

*Who Is It?*

This poem is about being a woman...to be whomever I wanted, to throw caution to the wind and dance. Women are so many things to so many people. We are everywhere doing everything which is why we are so filled with emotion. Women drive so many things in the universe, keeping everything on its proper course; after all, we are the bearer of that marvelous gift called "life".

-1995

# Who Am I?

When I was a little girl,
I was a beautician
A movie star
Whatever I wanted to be

When I grew older,
I was a singer
A model
A dancer
Whatever I felt I could be

Now, I am an adult,
I am anger but not hate
Pain but not wounded
Frustration, but not defeat

I am love
I am courageous
Aggressive
Strong
I am everything I can be

Who am I?

Every Woman!

Wow, this poem dealt with me as a young woman not knowing who I was or what I was supposed to be. On the brink of a failed marriage, a job loss, and being broke, I was in a state of chaos. I could not face life or my issues, and I had become someone I didn't even recognize. The bottom line was if I didn't know, then surely, no one else would. I had to be able to look into the mirror and find me.

-1995

# Who Is It?

*When I look into the mirror*
*Who is it that I see*
*A form without a face...Could this be me?*

*When I look into the mirror*
*Who is it that I see*
*A girl, a woman...Who could it be?*

*When I look into the mirror*
*Who is it that I see*
*I don't recognize the face before me*

*When I look into the minor*
*Will I ever know, who I am*
*And where I'll go*

*When I look into the mirror*
*Who is it that I see*
*I guess no one will ever know but me...*

# "Love"

I write a few poems about love, happiness, and finding that soul mate or companion. Well, it's partially because I am a true romantic at heart although at this time, I can barely remember what it felt like to be in love or be loved. In fact, I don't know if I ever really was …interesting, given the fact that I was married once a long time ago in a far away place…oh! I digress…LOL!

My soul dances when I think of what it must be like or I see people who look like they know. I rejoice in knowing that one day it could happen to me and I will keep hope alive! This poem is ode to that love supreme.

-2003

# An Affair of the Heart

*If my heart dances when I look at you,*
*It's because it hears the beat of a melodic drum*

*If my heart sings when you smile,*
*It's because you struck the right chord*

*If my heart laughs when I think of you,*
*It's because you bring joy*

*If my heart cries in front of you,*
*It's because you will catch every tear that falls*

*If my heart sleeps beside you,*
*It's because you are the sweetest melancholy*

*If your heart touches mine,*
*It's because you have found the key*

*If my heart opens,*
*It's because you have found me*

*If I give my heart to you,*
*It's because God says so…*

This very short poem was simply about finding love and losing love in what seemed like the same day. It's funny how you meet someone, fall in love, and then, the next thing you know, LOVE HAS LEFT THE BUILDING!!!! And you look up like, what the hell just happened?? Where did it go?

-1995

# Where did you go?

*I saw your smile and felt your touch*
*I kissed your lips it meant so much*

*I looked into your eyes*
*And saw the sunrise...*

*I know you were real*
*Where did you go?*

*Please tell me, I want to know*
*Were you just a dream? What could this mean?*

*I know you were real,*
*Cuz I can feel*

*Where did you go?*

This poem was written after attending a wedding. I had just gone through a separation in my own marriage and wondered if I would EVER stand at the altar of matrimony again. It was a bitter sweet day.

-1995

# I Remember

*I remember when I stood where you stand*
*When I said what you are saying*
*When I listened to what you are hearing*

*And…*

*When I thought forever and ever meant a lifetime*

*And now…*

*Once again, I walk alone, hoping to one day have another chance to stand*
*where you have stood*

I wrote this as my introduction to that beautiful black man who will sweep me off of my feet with his smile, protect me with his arms, and warm me with his heart…the man that would see my soul and not myself and love me no matter what. Oh! I must mention this poem began as a conversation with a friend who is quite poetic. Thanks E!

This is for the one I would give my friendship and all of my love to…then finally the one I will utter those 3 beautiful words to "Yes! I do".

-2002

# These 3 Things

---

*Hello handsome ebony king*
*It is with an unspoken sentiment I bring…*

*I bring you warm wishes from the heart, as I have had for you from the very start*
*The start of this awesome journey in the spirit of friendship, joy and love*
*Of these 3 things, the greatest, I have plenty of…*

*The others are a result of the one that shines as bright as a star, leading me to my destination*
*And without hesitation…I will go…*

*Go where you lead, follow your footsteps*
*Take your hand, as we stand…where no man can put asunder*

*Hello handsome ebony king*
*It is with spoken sentiments I bring*

*These 3 things*

This poem was written about that special time in a woman's life. I thought to myself, there is no greater gift than a child. I wrote these words so that if I was blessed to be a mother someday, my child would know just how special they are and how much I love them.

-2002

# My Greatest Gift

*They say love is like a river that runs on and on and on…through seasons that change*

*They say love is a gift that can't be measured by its size or contained*
*I say to love is to live and to live is to grow…my love for you allows me to live and as you grow , I grow and together our love is endless*

*We are like the river Nile that flows over many rocks,*
*You are a gift that is priceless not to be stored in a box*
*So I'll share you with the world but just know…the love I carry in my heart*

*Until life we depart, is my greatest gift, for it goes on and on and on…*

This poem is simply about disappointment. You meet someone you are really feeling and the vibe is right; and, you get to thinking hmmm… maybe this might be something…could you be falling for this person? I mean after all you really like each other, it's like the notes of a beautiful piece of music and then, all of a sudden, E Flat! …the Blue Note.

-2008

# The Blue Note

*Why do I hear this note in my ear?*
*The melody is slow the words I don't know...*
*It dances in my head, touches my soul,*
*It moves my feet with every heart beat...*

*The Blue Note*

*Why do I hear this note in my ear?*
*What does it mean? Have I been in this scene?*
*Other notes came along and soon there was a song...*

*The Blue Note*

*Why do I hear this note in my ear?*
*The stage has been set, there is some regret...*
*The piano plays a melody I wrote, one key...*

*The Blue Note*

Ahhh! What can I say about this poem...well Denzel said it best, "Mo betta makes it Mo betta" LOL! This is for the one that just makes you wanna holla...um hmmmm.

-2008

# Mo betta You

*Your smile is like the sun big and warm….*
*Your skin is like butter smooth and calm...*
*Your eyes like onyx full of mystery and intrigue…*
*Mo betta you*

*Your spirit is a melody gentle as a breeze…*
*Your passion moves me like the waves on the seas…*
*Your voice so full of strength and honor…*
*Mo betta you*
*You are quite the charmer*

*Your humor makes me smile…*
*Soooo stay a little while …*

*Cuz…*

*Mo betta you*

*Plus…*

*Mo betta me*
*Is my mo betta recipe*

I had been praying for a good man to come into my life, but it was when I learned what to pray for specifically that I met this man. I stopped praying for what I *wanted* and prayed for what I *needed*. He is one of the most unselfish, patient (with me...LOL!), and loving men I have ever met. He makes me laugh and loves me unconditonally. No relationship is perfect, but I believe in my heart that He is meant for me. He's my beautiful one and I love me some him!

-2009

Mel, this one's for you ;0)

# Beautiful One

*Your skin is like chocolate*
*Your smile is like the sun*
*Your eyes are like almonds,*
*Your lips are as smooth as they come*

*You are the beautiful one…*

*Let me love you*
*Open you heart and let love begin*
*Open your soul and allow trust to come in*

*You are the beautiful one…*

*I don't care what past you've come from*
*I only want to know the man you've become*
*I want to know where you are going, which road you will take and what path will you make*

*You are the beautiful one…*

*Wait for me, I'm going too, there's room for me and for you*
*Open your heart and let love begin*
*Open your soul and let me come in*

*You are the beautiful one…*

*You are MY beautiful one*

# "Friendship"

The Quilt

I have been blessed with a colorful garden of friends over the years. My Mother used to say to me, "Gertie pick and choose your friends wisely". She would be proud. I have been blessed to find a few good friends; it's like winning the lottery.

-2005

# The Quilt

*Friendships are like the many patches that make up a quilt, they connect at different points, they come in different patterns, shapes, and colors*

*You are the one common thread that ties them all together side by side you stand through any kind of weather...*

*When the last thread is sewn, you end up with a beautiful creation When it's cold it will keep you warm, when you are tired it comforts you, and protects you in a storm It can travel wherever you go and makes you feel at home for sure...*

*Friendships are like quilts, made up of ties that bind so they withstand the test of time It's good to have had at least one then to have had none...*

*You are the one common thread that ties them all together Side by side you stand through any kind of weather...*

# "Beloved"

A Jewel

Who Are You?

Georgie Girl

I wrote this poem for my Mother, Sophie R. Elam. She and my Father adopted me when I was about 13 months old. She wanted a girl and was not able to have any more children. I was born with a defect of my right eye, so it drooped a little. When I was a little girl, she knew children would tease me about my eye *and they did*, and she also knew they would tease me about being adopted *and they did*. My mother had a way with words so she prepared me for what she knew would come. She would say, "you tell them you are special and my Mother chose me, yours didn't have a choice." As I grew older I found humor in those words. She always told me I was no different than any other child because I was adopted. She truly was a gem and for that I thank her for choosing me and giving me the best childhood I could ever have dreamed of.

-2005

# A Jewel

*I know you didn't bring me into this world,*
*But you brought the world to me*

*If you had not chosen me, who knows where I might be*
*You made a sacrifice and dedicated your life…*

*You taught me to always be honest and to never lie,*
*But to walk tall and hold my head up high*

*You said no matter what trials life might bring, always pray*
*For God can fix anything…*

*Oh yeah and one more thing…*
*"God don't like ugly and he ain't too pleased with pretty"*

*You were a jewel in this treasure box of life!*

*Like the Ruby you sparkled with vibrancy*
*Like the Sapphire you roared with confidence*
*Like the Emerald your birthstone, you walked like royalty full of Grace*
*Like the Pearl you were guarded and not quick to open up*
*Like the Diamond you lit up the room with your smile and rich laughter*
*Now like the color of night, you are like the Onyx*

*Yes this chapter of your life on earth has ended but your book is not finished*
*The angels are rejoicing in what Jewel like the Opal, they have found*

*I hope that what you see from where you are is as bright as that North Star*
*I hope when you look down on me, you are pleased with the person you see*
*I can only hope to bring to this life, a portion of what you brought to me*

This poem is filled with a lot of emotion and is very personal for me. The reason I wrote this poem was because my mother suffered from Dementia and Alzheimer's disease, and I watched her mind progressively deteriorate in what seemed like over night. The next thing I witnessed was her physical health spiraling down until a wheelchair held her body. This disease also affects the people who love and care for that person. The disease robs you of your identity; you don't know who you are, where you are, or what time of day or night it is. You just live in a capsule.

At the time I wrote this poem my mother was alive, but she has since passed on, on August 30, 2005. She was a beautiful tree once full of life, grace and standing tall; now, she will rest in an eternal garden. I will miss her for the *rest of my life*. Some people said after the funeral, "Oh you still have the memories of your Mother" as they went on with their lives. And, there I was to grieve alone, but I know they meant well. You only get one, and when they are gone, they are gone.

The grief you feel from losing a parent, the pain that burns your chest, and the void in your heart is indescribable. So many times in my life, I've longed to talk to her and have her give me some of her sage advice and share her infinite wisdom. There is a season for everything, a time to live and a time to die. I thank God for lending her to me for all these years to nurture, teach, protect, love and educate me. If I had my own choice to pick a Mother, I would have chosen her. I am eternally grateful for her gift of life.

-2005

# Who are you?

*Who are you?*
*Did you come in the night, or*
*Was it daylight?*

*I can't remember your face, this house, this place*
*I was not expecting you; you just dropped in and...*
*Decided to stay awhile rendering the antics of a child*

*You brought fear, confusion and pain... Is there no sunshine after the rain?*
*I wish you would leave, for your purpose I can't conceive*
*Now look what you've done, I can no longer run*
*From the darkness that covers the windows to my soul*

*Who are you?*
*Did you come in the night, or*
*Was it daylight?*

This poem was inspired by my childhood nickname my Father gave me: "Georgie Girl". I never understood how he came to giving me this nickname, but he always called me by that name. He was a sweet, gentle and quiet man. I don't think I ever told him how much I loved him and how much he meant to me, but somehow I think he knew. I blamed my Father for splitting up our family because of his addiction to alcohol. It was not until I was almost an adult that I realized it was an illness and began to understand the dynamics behind how he got there, but by then, unfortunately, it was too late and he passed before I could apologize.

-2005

# Georgie Girl

*Georgie Girl is what you called me when I was a little girl*

*You would take me to the park, push me in the swing and buy me just about everything*

*We would sit on the porch for hours and watch the storm as it passed over*

*We would smile at the rainbow that would soon follow*

*That's when life was good*

*We would walk to the spring to get water and sing all the way home hand in hand, father and daughter*

*You closed your eyes and I said goodbye, I never thought you would make me cry*

*I hope that you are finally at peace, for those childhood memories seem to never cease...*

# Biography

Gertie Allegra Elam was born in Richmond, Virginia. She attended Virginia Commonwealth University and the Medical College of Virginia. She holds a Bachelors of Science degree in Healthcare. Gertie has been writing poetry over the last 20 years and has been a contributing writer on a few articles for an online fashion magazine, Eden Magazine. *A few of my Favorite Things* is her first publication. She is currently employed in the Telecommunications & Government Contracting industry in Washington DC.

Photographed by: Shea Ali Dixon, My View Point Photography

Make-Up by: Ontaeia for MAC

Hair by: Stacie for Stella Bleu'

A healthy mind gives way to a healthy body,

A healthy body gives life to a healthy *soul,*

And...

A healthy *soul* attracts a kindred spirit...

G. Allegra Elam

www.ingramcontent.com/pod-product-compliance
Lightning Source LLC
Chambersburg PA
CBHW031933080426
42734CB00007B/660